THE
MANDALAS
Colouring Book

CARLTON BOOKS

THIS IS A CARLTON BOOK

Published by Carlton Books Ltd
20 Mortimer Street
London W1T 3JW

Copyright © 2014 Carlton Books Ltd

A CIP catalogue record for this book is available from the British Library

10 9 8 7 6 5 4 3 2 1

ISBN 978-1-78097-591-7

Printed in China

Picture credits: Shutterstock and Thinkstock